GRANNY WILL YOUR DOG BITE
AND OTHER MOUNTAIN RHYMES

GRANNY WILL YOUR DOG BITE

AND OTHER MOUNTAIN RHYMES

by Gerald Milnes

Illustrated by Kimberly Bulcken Root

Alfred A. Knopf New York

To the memory of
Currence and Minnie Hammonds,
mountain people with old-time ways
who passed them on
G. M.

To Thomas and Peggy Nichols Root,
who introduced me to mountain music
K. B. R.

THIS IS A BORZOI BOOK PUBLISHED BY ALFRED A. KNOPF, INC.

 Published in the United States by Alfred A. Knopf, Inc., New York, and simultaneously in Canada by Random House of Canada Limited, Toronto. Distributed by Random House, Inc., New York. Manufactured in the United States of America. 0 9 8 7 6 5 4 3 2 1
Designed by Eileen Rosenthal

Library of Congress Cataloging-in-Publication Data: Milnes, Gerald. Granny will your dog bite and other mountain rhymes. Summary: A collection of rhymes about various aspects of mountain life.
1. Mountain life—Juvenile poetry. 2. Children's poetry, American.
ISBN 0-394-84749-0 ISBN 0-394-94749-5 (lib. bdg.) [1. Mountain life—Poetry. 2. American poetry]
I. Root, Kimberly Bulcken, ill.
II. Title. PS3563.I443G73 1990 811′.54 88-27350

AUTHOR'S NOTE

One fall afternoon in 1975, I stood with a fiddle under my arm and knocked at the door of a small, red-roofed house in the mountains of central West Virginia.

"Come on in," answered an old man, without asking who I was or what I wanted. Inside, I introduced myself to him and his kind-faced wife as the boy who, with his bride, had moved onto the old farm on Indian Lick, across the river.

"We're glad you came," the old man said. "Just throw your hat on the bed, spit in the fire, sit down on your fist, lean back against your thumb, and make yourself at home."

The old woman gave him a scornful look. "He's always actin' the fool," she apologized. "Have you had your dinner?"

I nodded.

"I heard that you could play a banjo and sing old songs," I said to the old man. Suddenly he looked modest.

"Oh, I can't play much—and I traded my singer for a whistler, but now I can't whistle. Can you play a fiddle?"

"A little."

"My uncle was a good fiddler," he said. "Upon my honor, he was hard to beat. He played 'Fine Times at Our House' the best you ever heard. And 'The Barkin' Squirrel' and 'The Wild Goose Chase.' Can you play 'The Devil in the Woodpile'?"

I didn't know it.

"Then just play me 'Sally Goodin.'"

I got the fiddle in tune and sawed a few notes of it. The old man smiled at the old woman. When I got to the fine part, she sang,

Blackberry pie and huckleberry puddin',
Give it all away just to see Sally Goodin.

He jumped up and hit the floor dancing.

After three or four more tunes he said, "I think I'll play you one on my old jo-head." He reached an old banjo down from its hook on the wall. "I'll play you a little bit of 'Sugar in My Coffee.'"

"When my mother was ninety years old, she got out of a sickbed to dance when he played that." The woman smiled.

And so the afternoon went. I could hear the old woman frying potatoes and making biscuits in the kitchen, humming tunes all the while. I said that as it was getting late, I thought I'd better be going.

"Oh, what's your hurry? Don't rush off," said the old man.

"Stay and have a bit of supper with us," said the woman, from the kitchen door. "It's not much, but you're welcome to it."

The old man gave thanks for the meal, then said, "Now just reach and get what you want and make yourself at home. I never did believe in such a thing as strangers."

After a fine supper he said, "I want to try out a riddle on you." One led to another and later, as the wood stove crackled, I sat spellbound as he sang a long old song about a highwayman and a lady. The old woman helped him remember the words. Then she sang "Pretty Polly" and spoke of a friend who wanted it sung over his grave.

He went back to playing the banjo and telling jokes, then sang "Old Man, Old Man, Can I Take Your Daughter" and threw back his head and laughed. He asked me to fiddle "Ryestraw." Next it was "Leather Britches," and we played "Sourwood Mountain" and "Liza Jane" together while the old woman sang. Before I knew it, it was midnight and I said that I absolutely had to leave.

"Oh," he said. "Why don't you just stay the night?"

"I really have to go."

"Well," he said, "you ought to stay the night. If we can't find an extra bed, we'll just hang you up on a peg!"

He was "actin' the fool" again.

We said our good-nights, and as I went out through the yard they called from the door, "Now you hurry and come back."

I had to go, but in some ways I never left.

Something special happened that night. I'd found the chain that links us to the distant past. It was the start of a journey that leads over hills and up hollows, to the homes of singers and fiddlers, to cakewalks and square dances, to fairs and festivals, and to front porches and warm kitchens. It leads wherever the spirit still moves the fiddles and banjos to play away the night, old songs to fill the air, and people to make their own fun.

The rhymes, songs, and riddles in this book were heard on that memorable day and night in 1975, and during hundreds of visits with these and scores of other resourceful folks. Through the years my children have been entertained by these rhymes in that warm little house and other homes in West Virginia. The rhymes, by unknown authors, have been passed down through an oral tradition that is kept alive by folks who are still using them in the traditional way. It's a privilege to know these people, these present-day links of the old chain, and to have had these rhymes passed to me. It's a pleasure to pass them on to you.

Gerald Milnes

Currence and Minnie Hammonds, Clyde and Lucy Case, Cletus and Lou Johnson, "Old Man Lee" Triplett, Maggie Hammons, Melvin and Etta Wine, Mose Coffman, Russell and Cecelia Higgins, "Lefty" Shafer, Bill Major, Sherman and Allene Hammons, Ernie and Mabel Carpenter, Jimmy and Gatha Dowdle, Dave Bing, Sylvia O'Brien, and Jenes Cottrell. Thank you.

Somebody stole my old black dog,
I wish they'd bring him back;
He runs the big hogs over the fence
And the little ones through the cracks.

Squirrelly he's a pretty thing,
He carries a bushy tail;
He eats up all of Mossie's corn
And hearts it on the rail.

Took old Sager out a-huntin' one night,
Blind as he could be;
He treed eleven possums up a sour gum stump,
I'll be danged if Sager can't see.

MERCANTILE

I had an old horse, his name was Bob,
I shelled out corn and fed him on cobs;
His legs were skinny and his back was flat,
And on them cobs I made Bob fat.

I took Bob down to the railroad track,
And I tied my banjo on his back;
Gave him a kick and I hollered Whoa!
And away went Bob with my old banjo.

I had another horse, his name was Dobbin Gray,
His legs were made of corn shucks, his body out of hay;
I saddled him and bridled him and rode him into town,
And along came a windstorm and blowed him up and down.

As I was going up the heeple steeple,
There I met a heap of people;
Some were knicky, some were knacky,
Some were the color of brown tobaccy.

Granny will your dog bite,
Your hen peck, your rooster fight,
Your turkey walk a fence rail?
No child, no.

Granny will your dog bite?
No child, no child;
Daddy took his biter off
A long time ago.

Poor old Piedy
She died last Friday;
The poor old creature,
The turkey buzzards have eat her.

How do you spell turkey buzzard?

T u izzard turkey,

T u izzard *y*;

T u izzard turkey buzzard,

Going to fly.

How in the world did the old folks know
That I liked sugar in my coffee-o?
I'll tell you how that they found out,
They found sugar in the coffee spout.

Me and my wife and a stump-tailed dog
Started across the river on a poplar log;

The log went down and I went in,
Round and around we'd go again.

If I had a cow
and she had a calf,

She'd give buttermilk—
wouldn't I laugh.

I plant my corn all in one row;
I feed it all to the horny ewe;
The horny ewe is a very fine sheep,
And the rest of the flock is hard to beat.

Charley he's a fine young man,
Charley he's a dandy;
Charley likes to go to town
To buy the ladies candy.

Over the river to feed my sheep,
Over the river to Charley;
Over the river to feed my sheep
And gather in the barley.

I don't want your weevily wheat,
I don't want your barley;
All I want is a little flour
To make a cake for Charley.

Hookety-crookety, high-gang Sal;

Every year clippety, what's that now?

The sly old crow was sitting in an oak,
Watching a tailor cutting out a coat;
Hey-ho said the sly little crow,
Caw caw
Fol da riddle riddle ly de o.

Wife bring here my arrow and a bow,
So I can shoot this danged old crow;
Hey-ho said the sly little crow,
Caw caw
Fol da riddle riddle ly de o.

I shot and I shot but I's unlucky somehow,
'Stead of shootin' the crow, I shot my neighbor's sow;
Hey-ho said the sly little crow,
Caw caw
Fol da riddle riddle ly de o.

Wife bring here some brandy in a spoon,
Because this old sow's in an awful tune;
Hey-ho said the sly little crow,
Caw caw
Fol da riddle riddle ly de o.

The little bell rang and the big bell tolled,
The little pigs cried for the old sow so;
Hey-ho said the sly little crow,
Caw caw
Fol da riddle riddle ly de o.

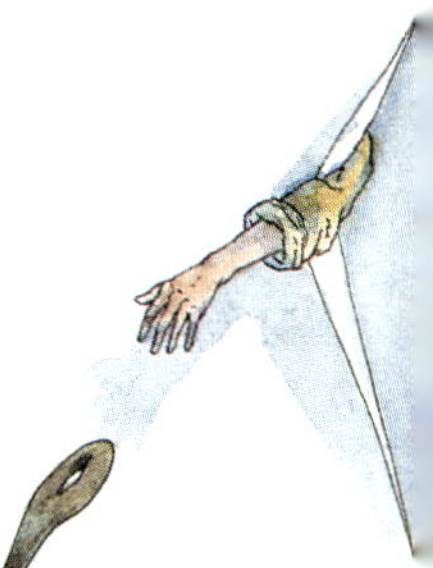

What're we going to do with the old sow's head?
Make the best cracklings that you ever put in bread.
Come a rippy dippy doey doey doey eye day
Come a rippy dippy doey doey eye doey o

What're we going to do with the old sow's tail?
Make the best iron wedge that ever split a rail.
Come a rippy dippy doey doey doey eye day
Come a rippy dippy doey doey eye doey o

What're we going to do with the old sow's snout?
Make the best ramrod that ever made a rout.
Come a rippy dippy doey doey doey eye day
Come a rippy dippy doey doey eye doey o

What're we going to do with the old sow's skin?
Make the best saddle that you ever rode in.
Come a rippy dippy doey doey doey eye day
Come a rippy dippy doey doey eye doey o

What're we going to do with the old sow's ear?
Make the best silk purse you ever held dear.
Come a rippy dippy doey doey doey eye day
Come a rippy dippy doey doey eye doey o

Dick stole the hoecake,

Ran through the meadow with it,

Hid it in a brush pile,

And swore he never meddled with it.

Old Dan Tucker went to town,
Riding a billy goat, leading a hound.
The hound dog barked, the billy goat jumped,
Threw old Dan Tucker a-straddle of a stump.

Old Dan Tucker came to town,
He drank a barrel of whiskey down;
The hoops, they broke, the barrel split,
Threw old Dan Tucker into a fit.

Old Dan Tucker, he got drunk,
Stepped in the fire and kicked out a chunk;
A red-hot coal got in his shoe,
Mercy sakes, how the ashes flew!

Smoke a-rising up the hill,
Brings more water to the mill.

Walkin' in the parlor,
Walkin' in a ring;
Watch the boy's finger
As he picks upon a string.

Walkin' in the parlor,
Walkin', I say;
Walkin' in the parlor
To hear the banjo play.

My old hen's a good old hen,
She lays eggs for the railroad men;
Sometimes eight and sometimes ten,
That's enough for the railroad men.

Cluck, old hen, cluck and squall,
You ain't laid an egg since way last fall;
Cluck, old hen, cluck and sing,
You ain't laid an egg since way last spring.

My old hen, she had a speckled foot,
She laid her eggs in a raspberry root;
She ruffled up her feathers to keep her eggs warm,
And another drink of cider wouldn't do us any harm.

Once was a soldier and he had a wooden leg,
No tobacco did he have and no tobacco did he beg;
Another old soldier, a sly old fox,
Always had tobacco in his old tobacco box.

Said the one old soldier, Will you give me a chew?
Said the other old soldier, I'll be danged if I do.
Quit your foolin' round and get to cracking rocks,
And you'll always have tobacco in your old tobacco box.

I went down to Grandfather's hall,
There I heard an old man call;
His beard was flesh, his mouth was horn,
And such a creature was never born.

The first to come in was Dad's old shoe,
It come in a-shufflin', too;
Come a ring-bow rattle and a jackstraw saddle
And a little boy paddled with a broom.

The next to come in was an old gray goose,
He tuned his fiddle and he cut loose;
Come a ring-bow rattle and a jackstraw saddle
And a little boy paddled with a broom.

I went to the river and I couldn't get across,
So I paid five dollars for an old blind horse;
He wouldn't go forward and he wouldn't stand still,
He jumped up and down like an old saw mill.

I went out to milk and I didn't know how,
So I hung my bucket on the horn of a cow;
The bucket, it swung and hit her on the jaw,
She rattled out a tune called "Turkey in the Straw."

Kitty Cole is gone to school,
Went down the road on a hump-backed mule;
Kitty Cole is gone to school,
If she don't get a learnin', I'll be fooled.

Davy, Davy, blue-eyed Davy,
He got drunk on chicken and gravy.

I had a dog and his name was Rover,
When he died, he died all over.

Leadin' up a goat a-straddle of a sheep,
Pattin' on the horns with the bottom of my feet;
Come a-walkin', Johnny Booger, won't you do do do,
Come a-walkin', Johnny Booger, won't you do?

I asked Johnny Booger for to mend my yoke,
He jumped to the bellows and up went the smoke;
Come a-walkin', Johnny Booger, won't you do do do,
Come a-walkin', Johnny Booger, won't you do?

I asked Johnny Booger for to mend my ring,
He didn't charge me nary a thing;
Come a-walkin', Johnny Booger, won't you do do do,
Come a-walkin', Johnny Booger, won't you do?

I asked Johnny Booger for to mend my plow,
He didn't charge me nothin' but an old milk cow;
Come a-walkin', Johnny Booger, won't you do do do,
Come a-walkin', Johnny Booger, won't you do?

Little minnow in the brook,
Daddy caught him on a hook,
Mama fried him in a pan,
Baby ate him like a man.

Oh the grasshopper leaned up against the fence,
And he laughed till his sides were sore;
The cricket said, You're laughing at me,
And I'll not play with you any more.

How do you spell grasshopper?

Hippety clinch,

Zeo zop,

Never stop

To get on top,

Over *e r*.

Grasshopper!

Oh Mama, my feet are sore
From dancin' over the puncheon floor;
I'll dance this reel and I'll dance no more,
I'll dance all over the puncheon floor.

I went down to old Joe's house,
Joe, he wasn't at home;
I ate up all of old Joe's meat
And fed his dogs the bones.

I went down to old Joe's house,
Joe was sick in bed;
I run my finger down his throat
And pulled out a chicken head.

I went down to old Joe's house,
He invited me in to supper;
He stubbed his toe on a table leg,
And stuck his nose in the butter.

What're we gonna do with the baby-o?
Wrap it up in a tablecloth,
Put it up in the stable loft,
That's what we'll do with the baby.

What're we gonna do with the baby-o?
Wrap it up in calico,
Take it down to its mammy-o,
That's what we'll do with the baby.

Back on the hill where the cowbells ring,
The rattlesnakes whiz and the yeabirds sing;
Sun's so hot our throats got dry,
You ought to have heard that jaybird cry.

Minnow on the hook,
And minnow on the line;
Fishin' with the girl
That they call Caroline.

Give me the hook,
And give me the line;
Give me the girl
That they call Caroline.

Chickens are a-crowing on the Sourwood Mountain,
Hi-ho a-deedle um a day;
So many pretty girls, you can't count 'em,
Hi-ho a-deedle um a day.

Up Buck Creek and down Salt Water,
Hi-ho a-deedle um a day;
Some old man's gonna lose his daughter,
Hi-ho a-deedle um a day.

I've got a girl, lives up the hollow,
Hi-ho a-deedle um a day;
She won't come and I won't follow,
Hi-ho a-deedle um a day.

Train on the island,
I thought I heard it blow;
Go and tell my Lulu girl
I'm sick and I can't go.

I went up on the mountain,
I did not go to stay;
I fell in love with a pretty little girl
And stayed till Christmas day.

Train on the mountain,
I thought I heard it squeal;
Go and tell my true love
How happy I do feel.

I went down in the meadow to mow,
A black snake took me by the toe;
I started to run and I run my best,
But I rammed my head in a hornets' nest.

I lost my glove yesterday,
I found it today;
I filled it full of rainwater
And tossed it away.

Mighty poor dog,
Needle eye, needle eye;
Mighty poor dog,
Needle eye o.

Can't catch a pet squirrel,
Needle eye, needle eye;
Can't catch a pet squirrel,
Needle eye o.

In and out the brier bush,
Needle eye, needle eye;
In and out the brier bush,
Needle eye o.

Can't catch a pet squirrel,
Needle eye, needle eye;
Can't catch a pet squirrel,
Needle eye o.

Old man, old man,
Can I take your daughter
To milk my cow
And carry my water.
Ha ha ha

Yes sir, yes sir,
Take her on behind you;
Take her up the hollow,
Where the devil can't find you.
Ha ha ha

Old man, old man,
Give me a chew of tobacco;
If you ain't got homemade,
Give me manufactured.
Ha ha ha

Ducks on the millpond,
Geeses in the ocean;
The devil's in the boys
When they take a notion.
Ha ha ha

Down in the hollow,
I thought I heard a fiddle sing;
Nothing but a little boy
Picking on a banjo string.
Ha ha ha

Here comes the old chimney sweeper,
He has but one daughter and he can't keep her;
So join your right hands and this broomstick step over,
And take a sweet kiss from your own true lover.

Over the river to see Betty Baker,
She won't work and the devil can't make her;
Over the river to see Betty Baker,
If she won't have me the devil can take her.

Raccoon's got a bushy tail,
Possum's tail is bare;
Rabbit's got no tail at all,
Just a little patch of hair.

Jaybird in a sugar tree,
Sparrow on the ground;
Sparrow told the jaybird,
Shake some sugar down.

An old sow had nine pigs under a rock.
The next morning they were all Woodcock's.

Little boy, little boy,
Where'd you get your britches?
Daddy cut 'em out,
And Mama made the stitches.

Leather britches, full of stitches,
Mama sewed the buttons on;
Daddy pushed him out of bed,
Because he had his britches on.

Patch upon patch,
With a hole in the middle;
Tell me this riddle,
And you'll get a gold fiddle.

Who's been here since I've been gone,
Old Uncle Ben with his nightcap on;
One shoe off and one shoe on,
In walked Sally with her blue dress on.

Dance all night with a bottle in your hand,
A bottle in your hand, a bottle in your hand;
Dance all night with a bottle in your hand,
Just before day, give the fiddler a dram.

Dance all night with the fiddler's girl,
Take her round and give her a whirl,
Up the river and round the bend,
That's all there is; this is the end.

INDEX OF FIRST LINES

Gerald Milnes — self-taught musician, writer, folklorist, and farmer—has been collecting rhymes, ditties, verses, and riddles from his West Virginia mountain neighbors since 1975. He has also written about West Virginia folklife, documenting the talents and traditional knowledge of the people of this region. He is now staff folklorist at the Augusta Heritage Center at Davis and Elkins College and lives with his wife and two children in Elkins, West Virginia.

Kimberly Bulcken Root is a graduate of the Parsons School of Design and has illustrated three books for children. She lives with her husband—also an illustrator—in Lancaster, Pennsylvania.